Storm in the Silence

a collection of poems

JAMÉ ROLLE

Storm in the Silence
Copyright © 2019 by Jamé Rolle. All rights reserved.

No part of this publication may be reproduced, stored in a retrieval system or transmitted in any way by any means, electronic, mechanical, photocopy, recording or otherwise without the prior permission of the author except as provided by USA copyright law.

The opinions expressed by the author are not necessarily those of URLink Print and Media.

1603 Capitol Ave., Suite 310 Cheyenne, Wyoming USA 82001
1-888-980-6523 | admin@urlinkpublishing.com

URLink Print and Media is committed to excellence in the publishing industry.

Book design copyright © 2019 by URLink Print and Media. All rights reserved.

Published in the United States of America

ISBN 978-1-64367-955-6 (Paperback)
ISBN 978-1-64367-954-9 (Digital)

21.10.19

Dedication

This book is dedicated to all the persons that believed in me when the world didn't…

Contents

Preface 9
Heart Break 11
Lust 13
The Escape 14
A Love 15
The Love 17
Heart Wrenching 19
Broken 20
The Mask 22
'Friends' 24
My Cigarette 25
But 27
Emotions 29
Pain? 30
Darkness 31
Rivers 33
Truth 34
My All 35
Bravery 36
Seconds 37
Promise 38
Hidden 39
From Home to House 40
Forever 41
If 43

Tick Tock 44
Tsunami 45
Acceptance 47
Mutant..49
Life..51
Battles 53
Pushed Away 55
Perfect 56
Cries..57
Killer 59
The Girl 60
His Silent Cry 64
The Attack 67
Conclusion..69

Preface

The inspiration for this book of poetry came from many sources, however, the main source would've been from the silent moments that I spent with myself pondering about my life. The moments in which I kept my own company and made my own happiness. This book is intended for those who suffer in silence, you're not alone, you will never be alone and to everyone else so that they may begin to understand what it is like to endure a 'Storm in the Silence.'

In order to understand what it means to communicate successfully in poetry, readers must develop both a foundation of poetry skills and understanding of the key elements critical to achieving success in poetry. I wrote this book to provide the necessary framework for conveying the essential skills in understanding and appreciating poetry. A good poet starts with developing a strong inter-personal relationship or connection with his or her readership. This book is the result of many years of facilitating, researching and reading poetry. It is my hope and desire that you will enjoy this book of poetry as I have enjoyed writing it.

Heart Break

Why her and not me
All that I have done
I have begged and pleaded
For your attention
In the least obvious of ways

I guess it wasn't good enough
My heart cracks
Every time I see you,
With her

The way you look at her,
The way you smile at her,
The way you talk to her,
The way you laugh with her,
It breaks my heart

Bit
By
Bit

I can't help the waterfall
That cascades down my face
I can't help the screams
That come from my heart
And echoes through my ears

The desolate cries
Of a broken heart
Shattering the deafening silence
In which I was stuck

But it's clear that you love her,
It's clear that you cherish her,
It's clear that she's your world,
It's clear that I will never be her

One more crack
And it will fall to the floor
At least then
The pain would end

And my heart would be no more

Lust

You won't even know it
Because I try not to show it
But you're dealing with
A lover/poet

I'll start speaking in tongues
And you won't even know it
Your body reacting to my words
Like I own it

Wanton desires
Awoken by the wolves of sensuality
Bitten by life's sin, no blood loss
Only humanity

Sinful desire,
Burning skin
Is what I feel
When I let you in

An embrace forbidden
But feels so right
An embrace I beg for
Every night.

The Escape

Cuts litter my wrists
Leaving blood in their wake
Face scrunched in pain
This is my only escape

This is what my life has become
Constructing a wall
To block everyone out
And act like I don't care at all

I want to scream and cry
I hate what I've become
Defeated by the thoughts of others
The only cure is to see my blood run

Maybe the time has come
Death is making its call
All it takes is one jump,
One cut,
One rope

To end it all.

A Love

So I say,
Give me a love
Like that of the sun and the moon
In which the sun

Gives up his life
Each and every night
So that his beloved,
The moon,
May live and breathe once more

But when love is present
Not all things work out
For when the sun is north
The moon is south

Oh how they wish
To collide
And become one
They can dream,

They can hope,
They can wish
Yet, not all dreams
Have a happy ending

However, this dream
Although it may only occur
Once every 18 years
That one day, those few seconds

Can be valued more than life itself
Those Few seconds bring everyone together
To gaze upon the beauty
Of their love

So once more I say
Give me a love
Like that of the sun and the moon
In which the sun gives up his life

Every single night
So that his beloved,
The moon
May breathe and live once more

A love
That if only for a few seconds
Everyone may come
And witness the true beauty of it

The Love

It's okay to feel
Alone, Lost
Or empty

For everything that is lonely
Eventually finds its company
Everything that is lost
Will be found

And everything that is empty
Will eventually get filled

I want to be wrapped
In your arms
Skin against skin
With our hands intertwined

Allow me the chance
To fall asleep
To the soothing lullaby
Of your heartbeat

The best love
I've come to realize
Is the kind of love that

Awakens the soul

The kind of love that,
Makes us reach for more

The Kind of love that,
Plants a fire deep within our soul
And brings peace
To our minds

That is the kind of love
That I wish to give.

Heart Wrenching

It's like walking
But not moving an inch
Dancing
but with no song

Singing
But with no sound
To your sorrows
You are bound

With the chains
Of your own mind
Lost in your own
Thoughts

Trapped in a cell
That you created
Through your down payment of worry

For,
A problem that you may never attain.

Broken

I'm broken
And you're broken too
But it's our broken love
That pulls us through

I've been thinking
About the stuff that I've been through
Didn't know I had been pushing you away too

All you ever wanted
Was to help me
But I didn't accept it
Its like I wanted these things to haunt me

But the truth is I was just hurt
I didn't want to be
Left alone in the dirt

Although you said that you
Would never leave
My trust is what you
Never had the chance to achieve

I'm broken
And you're broken too
But it's our broken love
That heals both me and you

The Mask

I cry,
I scream,
I wail
But never sleep
Covered in the broken shards
of promises,
No one seemed to keep

I wait
And I wonder
And I cry again
My broken soul
I try to mend

Then, I'm no longer alone
And the mask is on again
Laughing and smiling
My life is perfect
I have to pretend

That I am happy
As happy as can be
Act as if I'm jubilant all and everyday
Pretend my life is filled with clouds and rainbows
Not a single cloud is grey

"Are you okay?"
"Yes"
"Are you fine?"
"Of course"

Little do they know
That my
'Beautiful Smile'
Is forced

In the end
No, I'm not okay
Of course, I'm not fine
No matter how bright
My sun may seem to shine
I don't know how to feel joy
Or even happiness
I don't know why my life feels
Like a bottomless abyss

I try so hard
To cling to life
Although it's an everyday strife
No matter what the voices
Or people may say

I do hope that one day
I'll actually be okay.

'Friends'

My friends are liars
Deceivers and thieves
With every arrow and knife
I heave

They act as if they want the best
Act as if they care
Act as if I were to fall
They would all be there

They are superb archers
With the vision of an eagle
Maybe that that's why I never see when they hit
Only when they come running when
their blows make me feeble

Arrow after arrow
Slice after slice
For becoming their friend
This was the price

My Cigarette

As I unwrap you
I think of Christmas Day
The day everyone is filled with joy
And all sorrows are floated away

My heart rate quickens
As I place you between my lips
Your intoxicating smell, through my body
Rips

With you
I escape the horrors of reality
And snag a small piece of silence
I beg for this serenity

I inhale deeply
As your scent circles through my lung
Your unique taste
Lingers on my tongue

I wish that I hadn't
I allowed you in
Because the best fruits
Are always labelled forbidden

But
Being with you traps me
Yet
Simultaneously frees me

You trap me in a world of
Temporary bliss
Then you're gone
As the wind carries your breath's last wisp

Our meeting that are out back
And away in secret
Will forever be in my heart
And I will keep it

But

I would scream
But
My voice would be without sound
For to my cold broken soul
My voice has been bound

I would cry
But
Crying is for the weak
My happiness I've lost
But my dignity I will keep

I would fly
But
I have but one wing
Hanging onto life
By a rotting string

I would dance
But
The moves are foreign to me
Tripping over my feet
Sighing in defeat

The darkness that lived within

You feared
So, you left me alone
The weight I had to bear
All on my own

You stopped fighting
You let the darkness in
I had no strength to fight
So, the darkness did win

But when my jaw didn't go slack
And my eyes didn't go wide
It was then that you realized

That I had already died
Inside.

Emotions

I want to scream
I want to shout
I need to let all the emotions out

They're pent up inside me
I have nowhere to turn
They've got me on a rocky ride
Inside my emotions burn

I want to scream
I want to shout
I need to let all the emotions out

No one understands
The things I wish to say
They don't understand
The things that circle in my brain
Nor do they understand my pain

I want to scream
I want to shout
I need to let all the emotions out

Because in the end
They will destroy me
Without a doubt

Pain?

I saw a tree
Crying in the rain
A woman Hurting
But with no pain

Can time go by
And not make years
Can you lose your mind
And still feel sane?

How is it she can hurt,
But with no pain?
While a tree can stand alone
Crying in the rain

Darkness

At home I sit
As I continue to work
Oblivious to the darkness that
creeped in from every corner
And what may lurk

Eventually,
The darkness consumed the light
And everything familiar
Vanished from sight

The eerie silence
Cackled in my ear
But I could not move
I was paralyzed with fear

The voices started as whispers
Then they grew
The beings were small
But they grew too

Soon, the beings became giants
The whispers became shrieks
And soon my Chamber of sanity
Developed leaks

I laughed with the voices and roared with the beast
I don't know what was worse,
The fact that this is all a nightmare
Or the fact that I never went to sleep

Rivers

Joyful days are raindrops
That feed the riverside
While
Rivers ignited by sadness
Are fed with tears we've cried

It was once said
That the river of joy flows
To and for the just
But sorrow is a river too
And it runs on broken trusts

Bridges are built over these rivers
By the lessons that
We have learned
Including the bridges that have been washed away
And those that we have burned

For it is not the river of sorrow
But the river of joy that we yearn
I built my bridges over each of these rivers
Now it's your turn_

Truth

"I'm here for you"
Yet my tears stain
And coat my own shoulders

"I care for you"
Yet daily I pick up,
Dust myself off and keep on moving

"It's between us, I promise"
Yet my laundry lay scattered
Along the side walk

"I love you"
Yet I can't hear, feel, nor see you
Why wait for death
To say that you love me.

My All

I'm broken and bruised
Used and abused
A fragile porcelain doll
I've given life my all

They look at me under their nose
Standing in a not so grand pose
As I stumble and fall
Giving life my all

They leave me alone
In desolate places
7 billion people
14 billion faces

I've had enough
Time to go away
Maybe I wish not
To see another day

They no longer stand so tall
After I've really given life my all

Bravery

Words are tsunamis
But people splash them around
Like puddles

Poking at us
Chastising us
Because of our problems

We set ourselves on fire
To keep others warm
And instead of departing us peacefully
They throw our ashes into the storm

They throw us into the forest
To the wolves
But they should be certain
That we will come back

Never alone
Leading the entire pack

Seconds

One, two
I'm counting on you

Three, four
I'm at your door

Five, six
My feelings are in a mix

Seven, eight
I beg and plead for you to wait

Nine, ten
I guess this is the end

One, two
I miss you

Promise

She sat in the corner
All she could do is weep
Wrapped around the promises
No one seemed to keep

Her eyes dull and soulless
Like the night sky without a moon
Hoping that her end
Would come soon

Those who break her
Are the ones whom she seemed to miss
As she sits at her window
And makes a silent wish

She watched as the windowpane cried
And once more recited her wish
I wish the rain would go away,
For the rain is both a fading memory
And a distant promise

Hidden

Tears, pain, anger, hatred
Lost, afraid alone hurt
Used, abused and bruised

These are the burdens she carries everyday
Wishing hoping, and praying
That they will go away

With a smile on her face
And tears in her eyes
She greets every single
Passerby

Tired weary and ridden.
She want to get rid of the
Burdens that seem to be hidden

From Home to House

No emotion
Could possibly be worse than this
Where once was a home filled with laughter
Cheer and happiness

Is now a house filled with envy
Despair and loneliness
A home once vibrant active and rousing
Is now dull listless and like a bird with a broken wing

For which was once a home
Is now nothing more than a house

Forever

My heart is now
In so much pain
My tears are falling
Like heavy rain

I can no longer sleep
One full night
Now the bed bugs
Do bite

You broke my heart
And tore me apart
Were no longer together
What happened to forever

No one can redeem me
From the dark's grip, so tight
This time
There will be no light
And I can't fight

There's no reason to
Because there is no you
I loved you then
And I love you still

I made a promise
To always love you
And I always will

Although
We are no longer together
I still wonder
What happened to forever?

If

If I were a rose
With petals as black as ebony
And a green stem
Would the colour of my petals
Make me unworthy of being called what I am
Please tell me

If I were a rose
With petals of ivory
Would the colour of my petals
Be worth more than silver,
More than gold?

If I were just a rose
Sweet smelling and vibrant
And your mind was blind
Would my colour even matter at that time?

Tick Tock

Tick tock
Time is running away from us

Tick tock
It's leaving us all behind

Tick tock
The horror of knowing that you're dying every second

Tick tock
Time is running out

Tick tock
No, please, you can't be up so soon

Tick tock
Time's up

Tick tock
Is all I can hear

Tick tock
Tick tock

Tsunami

She was there when he needed her
Through thick and thin
He was a sinner
And yes, she did sin

She refused to believe
That he didn't love her
Thus, she was surprised when he left
Leaving her to suffer

All alone
And every night she cried
Missing him by her side

She missed
Each time that they used to kiss
Under shooting stars they made a wish

Together forever
Hand in hand through it
Forever, their language of love
Would be fluent

But it was all lies
Falling from the tongue of a snake
All the mental pain
Caused her to physically ache

She began to go down,
She began to wear
As the pain became too much
For her to bare

So she took the risk
She took the razor and slit her wrists

For she was the city
And
He was the Tsunami that destroyed her

Acceptance

I'm so fat
Why do I look like this
To be skinnier with long hair
Is all that I wish

Look at this,
Look at the size of me
As big as a house
Ten times (10x) bigger than a tree

I want to be beautiful
With golden hair
I want to go out
And be complemented everywhere

But wait,

What am I doing?
Trying to be perfect to the 'T'
Trying to please society
And not me?

People will always have a remark to make
No matter how I look
And that right there,
Was all that it took

I stood up tall, as bold as can be
It was beyond frightening
But
It was the first step into accepting me

Mutant

I've been mutated
My cells now wear a frown
Depression has infected
My very being

Suicidal thoughts,
Addictive cigarettes
Burning away my frontal lobe
Inducing pain

My heart pumps the pain
Out of my aorta
It then circulates through
My veins, arteries and capillaries

It mimics my cells
To avoid being attacked
And slips silently and swiftly
Past my valves never to flow backwards

Then I can feel it in my arms,
Legs and head
In my
Fingers, wrists and thighs

I'm a mutant
I've been mutated
Blood no longer runs through my vein
But has instead been replaced by pain

Life

Life is but a rose
None perfect
Yet
It remains a beautiful thing

Our lives are filled
With effervescent persons
Who are not always truthful

The thorns upon a rose
Represent the calamity
And the torture we endure
In our lives

It represents
The beauty of falling in love
But the unchanging stupidity
Of the dives

The multicoloured petals ranging
From black to red to white, to yellow
Represent
The beautiful and alluring things in our lives

As a young rose
Sepals hug the soft tender petals
These sepals represent those whom are in our lives
To protect us till it is our time to bloom

Battles

I wished not to fight
Yet you declared war
You whipped me
And threw me to the floor

You remained oblivious
That each blow received
Made me more robust than before

You chastised and bit at me
Suggesting I give up
But,
I will never give up

Nor will I give in
I will refuse to stand down
And let you win

If a fight is what you desired
Then a fight
Is what is required

Fight if you must
We will wrestle till dusk
For there is not enough room
In my mind
For the both of us.

Pushed Away

I helped you up
In return I was pushed down
You used me, abused me
And I made not a single sound

Then once again you fell
And were in need of help
I came to assist
I was told to go to hell

I leave as you fall once more
And once again are in need of help
I'm not sorry

But I thought that you should know
Now
I'm thinking about myself.

Perfect

Why would you want someone to be perfect
When you're not?
Why do you want persons to give their all
Then turn and say it's not enough

Why worry about the speck of dust
In his eye
When there is sand in yours?

Why expect him to be perfect
When you are nowhere near there
After all, life's not perfect,
So why should he be?

Cries

Just one cut
Then one more
Pit
Pat
Echoes
As blood drips to the floor

This is what I am subject to
Behind closed doors

Loud is my plea for help
Loud are my cries
Help is what I seek
Yet they continue to feed lies

"You're okay"
"You're fine"
"Just keep smiling"
How kind

They truly really are
To sell such a beautiful dream
I once believed them
But then the pain came

It tore away at my insides
And began to crawl upward again
Soon enough it will consume my mind
And I will become insane

Killer

Slice slice
Went your words
And splat went my heart

Boom boom
Went your words
As they tore me apart

Off went your gun
Pointed at me
In went the bullet
That caused my eyes to bleed

Off you went again
With a bullet to the head
Tore my mind wide open
And caused my thoughts to spread

I gave you the gun
And the seed grew root
You aimed the gun at me
But I still trusted you not to shoot

The Girl

Does it feel good?
Calling her a freak
When will you realize
That it makes her feel weak

I hope that you're satisfied
With yourself
Because now she's at home
And she's going through hell

She sits cross-legged in her room
As tears trickle down her face
She remembers all you ever had to say
Was that she was a waste of space

She holds out a razor
Wanting it to end
All she ever wanted
Was to have a genuine friend

The deeper the cut
The better she will feel
Do you feel jubilant
That her cuts may never heal?

Blood on her hands
Tears on her cheek
Wishing hoping and praying
That of death, she could get a peek

Your words cut her deep
Deeper than any knife
Yet you continue
To ruin her life

Week after Week
Year after Year
"I'm sorry"
Are the words that she's waiting to hear

Just to feel like someone's there to care
Or maybe someone feels regret
This could be that line
Between life and death

Years follow
And the apology still isn't said
The teasing intensifies
As voices fill her head

In the spur of the moment
Her decision is made
On her slender neck
She feels the cold unforgiven blade

One last slice
Will end it all
One more slit
And the angel shall fall

You could've prevented this
Save her from it
But you didn't
You just didn't know when to quit

Her fate had been decided
Your life you must now live with guilt
All because of the depression
That you built

It would've taken a simple smile
Or maybe even an apology
And right now
You wouldn't be hearing this eulogy

I hope that now your life is filled with guilt
Because you had your chance
But you ripped her to pieces
Not sparing her a second glance

She's infected
Forever does she sleep
As you sit there
And you continue to weep

She's gone, gone for good
And there's nothing left for you to do
Her smile,
Her face,
Her laugh,
Will forever haunt you.

His Silent Cry

There was a silent cry
In the middle of the night
Its source? A young man
Who screamed not from fright.

But screamed instead
From the pain within
From the wounds the demons created
And the battle that they began to win

In the end,
He could fight no more
He went to his armoire
And reached into his drawer

He took out his pencil
And prepared to draw
He was human
And this was his flaw

He pulled out his book
And stared at his old art
To his soul, mind, and body
They were now a part

And he began to draw
In his personal book
As he cried and screamed
And broke and shook

He drew horizontal lines
And vertical ones too
These were the only drawings
That he ever drew

He never used a crayon
And he never did dwell
On the fact that his drawings
Coloured themselves

Not two colours
Neither three or four
They knew one colour
And not another more

Yet he drew and he drew
And he continued to draw
Tears rolled down his face
As he chanted just one more

When it was all over
His whole page was coloured in
A beautiful deep red
That came from within

He put his pencil
Back into his drawer
Then took a seat
On the cold hard floor

The beautiful red colour
Began to seep
And soon consciousness
He could no longer keep

So he rested his head
Onto the ground
Where he continued to weep
But never made a sound

He closed his eyes
And he did weep
As he fell
Into an eternal sleep

In his head
His last thought being why
But it went unanswered
Because no one heard

His Silent Cry

The Attack

Pain, Despair and Rage
They visit again tonight
Feeding upon my broken soul
I could only put up a useless fight

Fear, Doubt and Anger
Just wont let me be
They wrap me in their cold embrace
Dragging me closer to insanity

My heart is frozen
Thus my feelings have gone numb
If only you could hear the voices
As they beg me to turn against everyone

I lock my thoughts and memories away
As the demons begin to win
The scars I bare outside are merely marks
From the wounds I have within

Captivity, Grief, and Sorrow
Have just arrived
Inside they made an ocean so deep
That no one dared to dive

But the demons

I began to dream dreams
That no mortal dared to dream before
To play with the demons inside
And open myself for more

Insanity, Desperation and Loss
Hold no secrets for me
My hope completely crumbled
Darkness see it's OPPORTUNITY

It plays twisted games with my soul
Then departs from me so quick
Then I drink the poison of my mind
And wonder why I feel so sick

This nightmare remains horrifying
As the fear and pain burrow deep
I have to wake up

Except

My eyes are wide open
And im not asleep

Conclusion

Some of these poems read like epic tales such as "The Girl", and others read like existential journal entries such as "Friends", while others portray my personal feelings when dealing with matters of the heart such as "A love". Writing this book of poetry tested my mental capacity like no other project has done before. This was because I had to analyze, dissect and formulate my writing skills to fit the pages and character of this book when I was composing these poems. Because poems have a deep underlying message, and often serve as analogies of important life events and how I felt at the time but more importantly they addressed the reasons why I wrote these poems. These poems were written to help the readers to understand the deep concepts of poetry without the need to explain them in any great details, but rather, allow these poems to touch your heart and soul.

www.ingramcontent.com/pod-product-compliance
Ingram Content Group UK Ltd.
Pitfield, Milton Keynes, MK11 3LW, UK
UKHW022217230426
12048UKWH00016BA/897